ONE FLEW OVER THE CUCKOO'S NEST

by
Ken Kesey

Teacher Guide

Written by
Pat Watson

Edited by
Heather M. Johnson

Note

The Signet 1995 paperback edition of the book, published by New American Library, a division of Penguin Putnam, Inc., ©1962 by Ken Kesey, was used to prepare this guide. The page references may differ in other editions.

Please note: This novel deals with sensitive, mature issues. Parts may contain profanity, sexual references, and/or descriptions of violence. Please assess the appropriateness of this book for the age level and maturity of your students prior to reading and discussing it with them.

SBN 1-58130-839-6

To order, contact your local school
supply store, or—

Novel Units, Inc.
P.O. Box 97
Bulverde, TX 78163-0097

Web site: www.educyberstor.com

Table of Contents

Skills and Strategies

Thinking
Research, compare/contrast,
analysis

Literary Elements
Characterization, simile,
metaphor, personification,
theme, allusion, symbolism,
inference, foreshadowing,
plot development

Vocabulary
Target words, definitions,
application

Speaking/Listening
Interview

Writing
Character sketch, poems,
response, review, Public
Service Announcements, TV
script, research paper

Comprehension
Predictions, cause/effect,
problem-solving, conflict

Across the Curriculum
Art—collage, papier mâché;
Drama—acting, script;
Music—appropriate
selections; Current Events—
newspaper/magazine;
Technology—Internet
research

Genre: fiction

Setting: mental hospital somewhere in Oregon; late 1950s

Point of View: first person

Themes: sanity/insanity, conformity/nonconformity, courage, good vs. evil, freedom vs. control, individuality, sacrifice

Conflict: person vs. person, person vs. "the system", person vs. self

Style: narrative

Tone: primarily pessimistic; moments of optimism

Date of First Copyright: 1962

Movie version: 1975, 133 min., rated R; directed by Milos Forman, stars Jack Nicholson, Louise Fletcher, Brad Dourif; won five Oscars—Best Picture, Best Actor, Best Actress, Best Director, and Best Screenplay

Summary

In a ploy to escape imprisonment on a work farm, Randle Patrick McMurphy cons his way into a mental institution. He encounters men who are dominated and intimidated by the cruel Nurse Ratched. McMurphy begins to challenge her authority and rally the other patients together. He annoys and makes fun of Nurse Ratched and attempts to change hospital policies. He gambles with, plans activities for, and ultimately inspires the other men by his courage. He befriends Chief Bromden, the narrator, who lives in his own foggy world, pretends that he cannot hear, and never speaks. The hostility between McMurphy and Nurse Ratched escalates into an all-out power struggle. Ratched insists that McMurphy and Bromden must undergo Electro-Shock Therapy when they defy authority and engage in a fight with attendants. McMurphy attacks Ratched when he realizes she has driven one of the patients to suicide. The plot culminates when Ratched forces McMurphy to undergo a lobotomy that leaves him unresponsive and uncommunicative. Bromden suffocates McMurphy and then finds the strength to escape.

Characters

Main Characters

Randle Patrick McMurphy: loud, strong, bold protagonist; represents overt sexuality and freedom; chooses to be institutionalized in a mental hospital rather than serve jail time; determined to change the oppressive atmosphere of the hospital and to destroy Nurse Ratched's control of the patients

Nurse Ratched, a.k.a. Big Nurse: stern, unfeeling, manipulative antagonist; controls the mental institution; represents suppressed sexuality; mentally and emotionally emasculates the patients

Chief Bromden: narrator; large, half-Indian patient who has been in the hospital the longest; nicknamed Chief Broom; pretends to be a deaf mute; suffers from hallucinations; believes himself to be weak in spite of obvious physical strength

Other Patients

Note: Patients are categorized as Acute (there is still hope for a cure) or Chronic (there is no hope for a cure). Chronics are classified as Walkers (can still move independently), Wheelers (in a wheelchair), or Vegetables (unable to do anything for themselves).

Billy Bibbit: Acute; shy, repressed, thirty-one year old who stutters; intimidated, controlled, and made to feel guilty by his mother; commits suicide

Martini: Acute; "sees" things that aren't there

Cheswick: Acute; taken to Disturbed Ward after protesting institution's policies; drowns

Scanlon: Acute

Sefelt: Acute; epileptic who refuses to take his medicine

Fredrickson: Acute; takes Sefelt's medicine

Dale Harding: Acute; college graduate; serves as president of patient's council; dominated by his wife

Ellis: former Acute, now Chronic; left incapacitated by Electro-Shock treatments; remains in the same position most of the time

Ruckly: former Acute, now Chronic because of a mistake in treatment

Colonel Matterson: oldest Chronic; WWI veteran

Old Pete Bancini: Chronic; suffered brain damage at birth

George Sorenson: Chronic; former fishing boat captain; obsessed with cleanliness

Taber: former patient; subjected to "treatment" after questioning what is in his medication; used as an example to other patients

Other Hospital Staff

Dr. Spivey: primary doctor; easily manipulated; chaperones patients on a fishing trip

Miss Flinn: nurse

Nurse Pilbow: nurse; tries to wash away conspicuous birthmark; carries a crucifix

Mr. Turkle: night aide; assists McMurphy in planning the party on the ward

Geever, Washington, and Williams: black aides; loyal to Nurse Ratched

Others

Candy and Sandra: friends of McMurphy; prostitutes (Candy is instrumental in Billy Bibbit's eventual death)

About the Author

Ken Elton Kesey was born in 1935. He moved with his family to a farm in Oregon in 1946. He later married Faye Haxby, and they had three children: Jed, Zane, and Shannon. He graduated from the University of Oregon in 1957 and studied creative writing at Stanford University from 1958–1961. Kesey worked as an orderly in the psychiatric ward of a VA hospital in California in 1961. While working there, Kesey began to have hallucinations of an old Indian sweeping the floors of the ward. These hallucinations later became the basis for Chief Bromden's character in *One Flew Over the Cuckoo's Nest*. Other works by Ken Kesey include the novels *Sometimes a Great Notion* (1964), *Sailor Song* (1992), *Last Round Up* (1994), and several children's books. He also produced two collections of shorter writings: *Kesey's Garage Sale* (1973) and *Demon Box* (1986). He died in November 2001.

Background Information

The following terms will help students understand the conditions of the patients in the mental hospital in *One Flew Over the Cuckoo's Nest*.

1. **mental illness:** a sickness or disorder of the mind ranging from mild emotional disturbances (neuroses) to severe personality disorders (psychoses). Early life experiences and various types of stress may increase the possibility that a person will have a mental illness.

2. **schizophrenia:** defined by the presence of one or more characteristic symptoms such as "hearing voices," hallucinations, irrational feelings of persecution, decreased or disorganized speech, or dulled emotions; can often result from a traumatic experience early in life

3. **clinical depression:** a mental disorder characterized by long periods of sadness and other negative emotions

4. **shell shock:** a nervous or mental disorder resulting from the anxieties of war

5. **obsessive/compulsive disorder:** having overwhelming thoughts followed by an irresistible impulse to repeat a certain action numerous times

6. **paranoia:** imagined persecution or the delusion of greatness

7. **phobia:** an unreasonable fear of a particular situation or object

8. **Oedipus complex:** a strong attachment by a male child to his mother

9. **emotional emasculation:** (figurative) to destroy the force of; weaken

10. **lobotomy:** the severing of certain nerve fibers connecting parts of the human brain; Antonio Moniz (1874–1955) introduced the prefrontal lobotomy operation as a therapeutic procedure in certain mental diseases. (used as punishment in the novel)

11. **electroshock therapy or EST (Electro-Shock Therapy, as it appears in novel):** the administration of electric current to the brain through electrodes attached to the head; induces unconsciousness and brief convulsions; primarily used to treat clinical depression (used as punishment in the novel)

12. **delusion:** a strong belief in something, despite evidence proving otherwise

13. **hallucination:** perceiving of or seeing something that is not there or does not exist

14. **Rorschach test:** a psychological test that measures personality traits based on the subject's response to 10 different standardized inkblot designs

Teacher Note

One Flew Over the Cuckoo's Nest contains profanity, as well as many mature topics and themes. These include references to gambling, rape, prostitution, homosexuality, assault, murder, suicide, alcohol/drug use, and sexual molestation. Please evaluate your particular class and community when teaching this novel. Consider discussing these topics with your students before they read and study this novel.

Initiating Activities

Use one or more of the following to introduce the novel.

1. Place the term "mental illness" on an overhead transparency. Brainstorm with students about the denotation and connotation of the phrase and their knowledge of treatment for the mentally ill.

2. Have students begin a Story Map (see page 7 of this guide) to use as they read the novel.

3. Show selected scenes from the movie *One Flew Over the Cuckoo's Nest* (rated R).

4. Students should keep a list of words and phrases that are made into proper nouns in the novel. Students should include their thoughts on why the author chose to capitalize them. (Suggestions: Electro-Shock Therapy, Group Meeting)

5. Have students research one of the terms listed in the Background Information on page 5 of this guide. Students should share their findings with the class.

6. This novel includes many sensitive subjects. Students should keep a journal to question scenes that disturb them most. Have students consider whether these subjects are exaggerated or not.

7. Students should make their own glossary of difficult words in the novel.

Story Map

Directions: Complete the story map below.

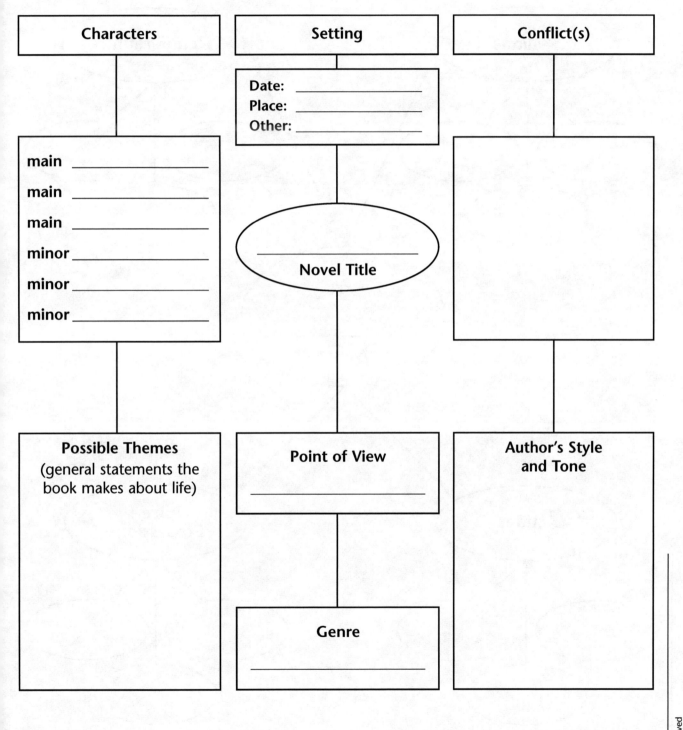

Characters

main _____

main _____

main _____

minor _____

minor _____

minor _____

Setting

Date: _____

Place: _____

Other: _____

_____
Novel Title

Conflict(s)

Possible Themes
(general statements the
book makes about life)

Point of View

_____

Genre

_____

**Author's Style
and Tone**

Character Web

Directions: Complete the attribute web by filling in information specific to a character in the book.

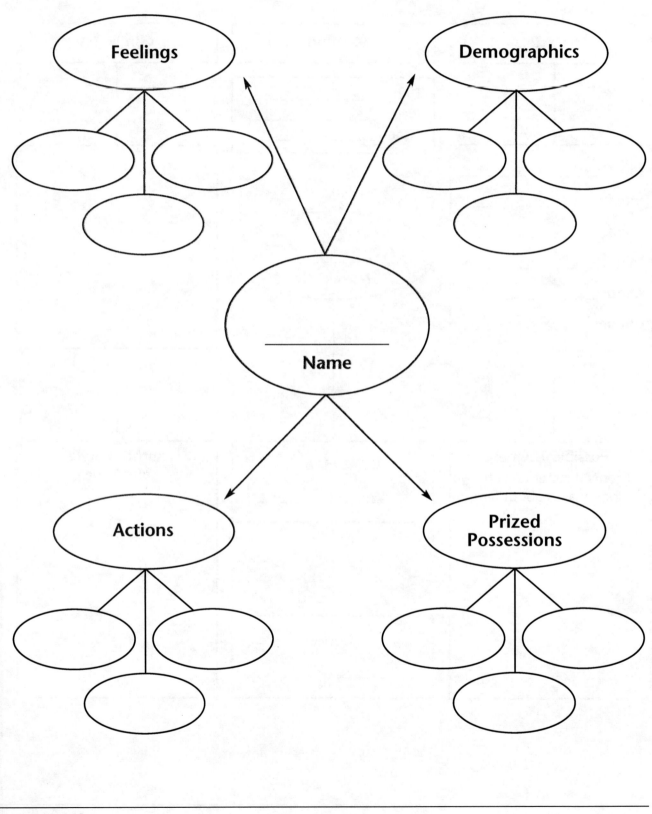

Character Chart

Directions: In the boxes across from each of the feelings, describe an incident or time in the book when each of the listed characters experienced that feeling. You may use "not applicable" if you cannot find an example.

	Nurse Ratched	R.P. McMurphy	Chief Bromden	Billy Bibbit
Frustration				
Anger				
Fear				
Humiliation				
Relief				
Hopelessness				

Cause/Effect

Directions: To plot cause and effect in a story, first list the sequence of events. Then mark causes with a C and effects with an E. Sometimes in a chain of events, one item may be both a cause and an effect.

Events in the story	Cause	Effect
1.		
2.		
3.		
4.		
5.		
6.		
7.		
8.		
9.		
10.		

Another way to map cause and effect is to look for an effect and then backtrack to the single or multiple causes.

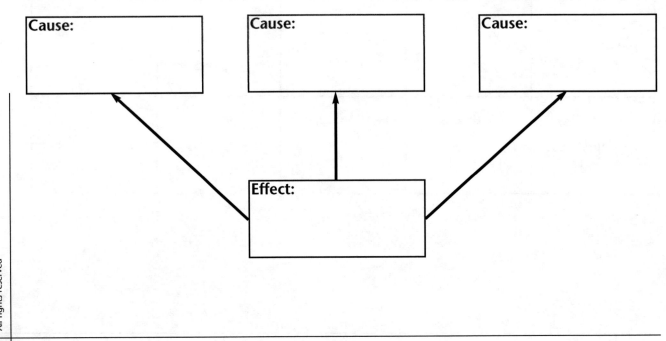

Foreshadowing Chart

Foreshadowing is the literary technique of giving clues to coming events in a story.

Directions: What examples of foreshadowing do you recall from the story? If necessary, skim through the chapters to find examples of foreshadowing. List at least four examples below. Explain what clues are given, then list the coming event that is suggested.

Foreshadowing	Page #	Clues	Coming Event

Graphing Plot Lines

Characters

Setting

Problem

Climax

Resolution

Building Action

Beginning

Note: *One Flew Over the Cuckoo's Nest* is replete with similes and metaphors. Examples of these and other literary devices are included in the Supplementary Activities of each section. Guide students to discover and list metaphors and similes from each section.

Part One, pp. 9–41

Chief Bromden, the narrator, is a patient in a mental institution where Nurse Ratched dominates both patients and staff. Bromden pretends to be deaf and mute and often retreats into a mental fog. McMurphy arrives and inspires the other patients with his charismatic personality. McMurphy quickly becomes a threat to Ratched's authority.

Vocabulary
cagey (10)
psychopath (18)
therapeutic (19)
bent (24)
philosophy (29)
neurology (31)

Discussion Questions

1. Discuss the characteristics of Nurse Ratched, Chief Bromden, and Randle Patrick McMurphy. *(Nurse Ratched, also known as Big Nurse, is the antagonist. She is efficient and organized, runs the hospital with precision, and completely dominates everyone with calculated, mechanical authority. Her outward smiles and assumed concern hide her manipulative, cruel nature. She delights in referring to her "successes" with difficult patients, e.g., arranging for them to receive Electro-Shock Therapy or other treatments. Staff and patients are afraid of her. Chief Bromden, the narrator, is a half-Indian who assumes the persona of a deaf mute because of circumstances throughout his life. He retreats into a mental fog when he feels threatened by others or when he must endure a humiliating procedure. His hallucinations about being in an Air Raid indicate former service in a branch of the armed forces. Randle Patrick McMurphy, the protagonist, is bold, loud, and manipulative. He faked insanity in order to be admitted to the mental hospital rather than complete his sentence at a prison work farm. McMurphy immediately convinces the other patients to gamble with him. He swaggers into the hospital and proclaims that the court has ruled him to be a "psychopath." From the first time he meets Nurse Ratched, he begins to undermine her authority and initiate changes in the institution and among the patients. pp. 9–18)*

2. Analyze the significance of Bromden's reference to the bird and the hunting dog. Note the importance of the "fog," a motif that recurs throughout the novel. *(At first, Bromden compares himself to the bird and the black hospital aides to the hunting dog. He experiences fear as a bird feels when a dog pursues it. He believes he will be safe as long as he remains hidden and still, but the aides capture him when he leaves the closet. He begins to hallucinate that he is in an Air Raid, and he retreats into a mental fog, where he then imagines a dog that is lost and afraid because it can't see. The fog symbolizes Bromden's retreat into his own world. When the fog lifts, he returns to reality. Kesey uses this hallucination to allude to the narrator's fear as he prepares to reveal the truth about the horrors of the mental institution. pp. 12–14)*

3. Examine the classification of the patients on the ward when McMurphy arrives. Discuss their individual characteristics. *(They are classified as Acutes, those who can possibly be "fixed," or Chronics, those who will probably remain in the institution for the rest of their lives. Acutes— Cheswick is the first one McMurphy greets; Billy Bibbit stutters; Dale Harding, a college graduate, is president of the Patient's Council. Chronics—Ellis remains perpetually in the same position with a look of horror on his face, and Ruckly unthinkingly holds a picture day after day. Both are former Acutes who are now Chronics because of hospital mistakes. Colonel Matterson, the oldest Chronic, is a WWI veteran. Bromden has been in the hospital the longest, since WWII. Old Pete is mentally retarded because of a brain injury at birth. Big George constantly washes his hands to avoid germs. pp. 19–28)*

4. Analyze the atmosphere in the mental hospital when McMurphy arrives and how he reacts. *(The atmosphere is oppressive. The men on the ward are restrained and controlled. The routine, beginning at 6:30 a.m., rarely varies, and the men subdue any overt laughter. They spy on each other, recording bits of information in the nurses' log book. The "spy" is rewarded with a star by his name and the privilege of sleeping late the next day. The exposed issues are then addressed in the Group Meeting [pp. 42–48]. McMurphy greets each patient, shakes his hand, and attempts to engage him in conversation. He jokes with the men and begins challenging Nurse Ratched and her rules. pp. 19–28)*

5. Analyze the metaphors Bromden uses to describe the hospital and the ward. *(Bromden refers to the hospital as the Combine and the ward as a factory for the Combine. The Combine represents the entire mental hospital, a well-organized, powerful machine designed to control everyone and everything. The ward is the Combine's factory, and its goal is to repair the mistakes of society. Nurse Ratched is the person in charge of the factory, and she delights in sending a docile, submissive dismissal back into the world. She is unconcerned if the treatment leaves the patient without initiative or diminishes his quality of life as long as he is no longer a problem to society. She considers Mr. Taber a "success" story because her prescribed treatment turned him from a manipulator into a meek, submissive man. Nurse Ratched guards her authority carefully, and when an admission arrives, her primary goal is to bring that patient into compliance with her routine and to keep her "machinery" operating smoothly. pp. 20–21, 29–30, 35–40; inference)*

6. Analyze Nurse Ratched's methods of control. *(Intimidation—Previous doctors only lasted between three weeks and three months before she found one submissive enough to suit her. She threatens the Acutes with the possibility of their becoming Chronics if they don't cooperate with staff policies; Fear—She chooses the three black boys as aides because of their hatred so patients will fear them. She ensures that patients see others taken away for "treatment" and then observe their condition when they return; Covert actions—She gives secret oral instructions to the three aides so no visitor will ever read written instructions. She hides her cruelty behind a fake smile. pp. 29–41)*

7. **Prediction:** How will McMurphy keep the hospital from running smoothly?

Supplementary Activities

1. Working in small groups, have students stage one of the following: (a) McMurphy's arrival to the ward, including pantomiming the body language of the patients (b) the Group Meeting (c) the initial conflict between McMurphy and Nurse Ratched.

2. **Similes**—I creep along the wall quiet as dust (p. 9); tiny pills that gleam like porcelain (p. 10); He opens out his nostrils like black funnels (p. 12); [Ellis] nailed…on the wall like a stuffed trophy; eyes…like blown fuses (p. 20); I feel like my veins are running ammonia (p. 31) **Metaphors**—black aides: black machinery (p. 10); patients: birds (p. 17); Chronics: machines (p. 19); McMurphy's hands: road map (p. 27) **Allusion**—Punch and Judy (p. 37)

pp. 42–69

McMurphy learns more about the patients and Nurse Ratched's control during a Group Meeting. He begins to gamble with other patients and places a wager that he can cause Nurse Ratched to lose her composure within one week.

Vocabulary
insubordination (44)
protocol (47)
prototype (48)
sadistic (56)
veritable (58)
ethereally (58)
benevolence (58)
matriarchy (59)
astute (61)
juggernaut (66)
impregnable (67)

Discussion Questions

1. Analyze the Group Meeting: its importance to Chief Bromden, Nurse Ratched's manipulation, McMurphy's reaction, Dr. Spivey's role, and its effect on the patients. *(Bromden is tempted to lose himself in the fog forever but wants to see how McMurphy reacts to the Group Meeting. As Nurse Ratched enters, McMurphy is the only one who will look directly at her. She manipulates the patients by openly discussing their problems and reading the reports her "spies," have written about them. Ratched also manipulates the patients into revealing secrets from their past. She demands absolute obedience to her rules. No information is kept private. After Nurse Ratched calls him by the wrong name, McMurphy implies that he knows how to stop her. He then sits quietly and intently observes the group therapy process. He senses the oppressive, restrictive atmosphere and attributes it to Ratched's control. Dr. Spivey's primary role is to talk about his theory of the therapeutic value of the group interaction. He is weak and ineffective and must depend on Ratched's help. The patients are subdued, fearful, and ashamed. McMurphy is puzzled at the patients' lack of courage. pp. 42–54)*

2. Discuss information in McMurphy's diagnostic report and what this reveals about him. *(He is 35 years old, has never married, received the Distinguished Service Cross in Korea for leading an escape from a Communist prison camp, but later received a dishonorable discharge for insubordination. He has been arrested on numerous charges, e.g., drunkenness, assault and battery, disturbing the peace, gambling, and statutory rape. This is McMurphy's first admission to a mental hospital, but he shows Dr. Spivey a reference in his report to repeated outbursts of passion that suggest psychopathic behavior. When Dr. Spivey reads a statement from the doctor at the work farm suggesting that McMurphy might be feigning insanity to escape the work farm, McMurphy assumes the body language of an insane man. pp. 44–46)*

3. Analyze the analogy of a pecking party. *(The patients are the chickens; Harding is the victim. When baby chickens are grouped together, they will begin to peck at a spot of blood on a chick and will eventually peck it to death. Others get blood on them in the process, and the "pecking party" begins all over again. Nurse Ratched's strategy is to exploit the patients' desire to please her by encouraging them to spy on and reveal secrets about each other. At a Group Meeting, she begins the "pecking" by revealing information about one of the patients and enticing the others to "peck" at his weaknesses. She emotionally emasculates a patient by embarrassing and shaming him before his peers. Another "victim" is then chosen. pp. 54–57)*

4. Examine McMurphy's conversation with Harding, noting their analysis of Nurse Ratched. *(McMurphy reflects on Nurse Ratched's ability to strike a man where he is the weakest by focusing on his sexual inadequacies. She takes away his self-esteem and masculinity and reduces him to a controllable, passive man. McMurphy denounces her pseudo persona as an angel of mercy and makes Harding recognize her for what she is—the controlling, malicious matriarch of the mental ward. Harding then reveals his true feelings toward Ratched and tells McMurphy he underestimates her. He compares the patients to weak rabbits who need a strong wolf like Ratched to keep them in*

their place. He implies that McMurphy is a rabbit who has not yet lost his sexual prowess, as have the other patients. McMurphy attempts to encourage the patients to believe in themselves and to quit being afraid. pp. 57–62)

5. Analyze the aftermath of the Group Meeting. *(The patients' emotions range from shame for failing to speak up to anger toward Ratched and dread that things will never change. Cheswick reveals his inability to follow through with confrontation. Billy Bibbit feels he can never change and contemplates suicide. All are intimidated by Nurse Ratched's questioning tactics and fear they will be labeled Potential Assaultive, sent to the Disturbed Ward, and eventually be referred for EST or surgical intervention. They cite Ellis, Ruckly, and Bromden as examples of what can happen to them if they challenge Ratched. McMurphy compares the Group Meeting to a prison camp, confronts the men with their own fears, and encourages them to rebel against Ratched. He wagers that he can conquer her with mind games. McMurphy admits that he got himself admitted to the hospital to escape the work farm. pp. 63–69)*

6. **Prediction:** Will McMurphy win the wager? How?

Supplementary Activity

Similes—[Pete's eyes] came clear as blue neon (p. 51); [needle] hung…like a little tail of glass and steel (p. 52); [hands creep] like white spiders from between two moss-covered tree limbs (p. 57) **Metaphors**—Doctor Spivey: ineffectual little rabbit (p. 59); Harding's face: a busted wine bottle (p. 60)

pp. 70–101

McMurphy learns more about the procedures on the ward and discovers that Chief Bromden can hear. Chief Bromden has fearful hallucinations. Tension between Nurse Ratched and McMurphy escalates as he attempts to cause changes in the ward. Dr. Spivey becomes McMurphy's ally.

Vocabulary
stoicism (73)
uncanny (75)
geriatrics (89)
infernal (95)
maudlin (97)

Discussion Questions

1. Examine evidence of Chief Bromden's mental illness and discuss his role as narrator. Do you think any of his "memoirs" are based on reality? *(He believes Big Nurse is able to set the wall clock at variable speeds, ranging from fast so she can shorten the patients' pleasurable experiences to slow, causing them to feel petrified and frozen in time. He believes she can pipe chemical gas and fog into the ward. Delusions indicative of mental illness include Bromden's depiction of the aides' ability to detain Santa Claus for six years and believing a patient is wired to pick up code signals. He hallucinates that the floor moves downward and stops in a huge room with machines and swarms of men deep in the ground. He thinks he sees a parade of people following the Public Relations man carrying his "trophies," i.e., withered heads of patients. When Bromden becomes terror-stricken, he retreats into a mental fog where he doesn't have to watch. His delusions and hallucinations attest to Nurse Ratched's oppressive control and the patients' fear of her. Answers will vary. pp. 70–72, 79–82)*

2. Analyze the symbolism of Bromden's hallucination of the torture of a patient named Blastic. *(When the men cut Blastic open, they find primarily rust and ashes, with nothing human left inside. This symbolizes the effect of the mental ward on the patients. Under Nurse Ratched's manipulation, they are slowly being reduced to robots that outwardly go through the motions of living but are dying inside. pp. 80–81)*

3. Analyze McMurphy's effect on the patients and staff. *(Patients: Bromden believes the ward is not really fogged the day McMurphy arrives. He concludes that the Combine has not yet gotten him. Things seem normal to Bromden, and he goes to sleep without sedation. McMurphy attempts to get the patients to loosen up. He begins to gamble with them, and they are pleased when he lets them win. He jokes with them. The patients are thunderstruck when they hear McMurphy singing the next morning because they have never heard anything like it on the ward. Staff: Because Nurse Ratched has suggested that McMurphy is a sex maniac, Nurse Pilbow is terrified of him. He frustrates the black aides. Nurse Ratched begins to show signs of stress, picking at the patient's weaknesses and lashing out in anger at the aides. pp. 71, 74–77, 83–89, 92)*

4. Discuss Dale Harding's role in the novel. *(He is the most rational patient on the ward and provides inside information for McMurphy, e.g., the music is always loud, and they are rarely allowed to hear the news. He cautions McMurphy that protesting the music or anything else will get him branded Assaultive. He clarifies ward policies for McMurphy. pp. 73, 94)*

5. Analyze the symbolism of McMurphy's shorts. *(His shorts are black satin covered with white whales with red eyes. The whales can be interpreted as symbolizing Moby Dick, the fierce white whale Captain Ahab is determined to kill. Allegorically, the story of the whaling adventure reflects the issues of human struggles. In this interpretation, Nurse Ratched represents Ahab, and McMurphy typifies Moby Dick. She is determined to conquer and destroy him because he represents a challenge to her control. In the book Moby Dick, the powerful whale symbolizes good and Ahab symbolizes evil. A whale also signifies untamed power, as does McMurphy, and the phrase "a whale of a good time" applies to many of his sexual conquests. His overt sexuality conflicts with Nurse Ratched's repressed sexuality, a recurring theme throughout the novel. The two engage in a power struggle when he implies that he is naked beneath the towel. She begins to lose her composure when he drops the towel to reveal his whale-covered shorts. McMurphy thinks he is winning, but Bromden knows Nurse Ratched will strengthen herself. pp. 87–92)*

6. Discuss the cause/effect of McMurphy's attempts to change ward policies and improve the atmosphere of the ward. *(Cause: He tries to get the music turned down. Result: Ratched refuses and accuses McMurphy of being selfish because the old men can't hear if the volume is lower. Cause: McMurphy asks to be allowed to take the card game to another room. Result: Ratched tells him there is not enough help. Cause: McMurphy enlists the help of Dr. Spivey. Result: The sound remains loud, but the patients receive permission to use the tub room for their card game. Cause: McMurphy and Spivey discover they are from the same school, where McMurphy directed plans for a carnival. Result: They begin to plan a carnival for the men, and the men become excited about a change in the monotony of their lives. Cause: Ratched recognizes McMurphy's manipulative strengths. Result: The power struggle increases. Cause: Bromden realizes Ratched is too big to be beaten and will eventually conquer them all. Result: He retreats into the safety of his mental fog. pp. 92–94, 101)*

Supplementary Activities

1. Have students draw a caricature of McMurphy in his whale-covered shorts.

2. **Similes**—[birthmark stain] runs like a river of wine down into a valley (p. 76); [shadow] as big as an elephant (p. 78); [wicker bag] like a semi behind a Jimmy Diesel (p. 87) **Metaphors**— Nurse Ratched's tongue: a chunk of slag (p. 90); McMurphy's dad: Frankenstein (pp. 100–101)

pp. 102–128

McMurphy continues to win money from the patients, and he grows more impatient with their lack of assertiveness. The fog that surrounds Chief Bromden increases. During the Group Meeting, McMurphy battles with Nurse Ratched over TV time on the ward. Nurse Ratched allows a vote on the subject, but again manipulates the situation using fear. McMurphy loses the vote but gains a moral victory. He leads the patients in a silent protest when Nurse Ratched thwarts his attempts at change.

Vocabulary
apathy (107)
interceptors (116)

Discussion Questions

1. Examine the significance of Chief Bromden's escape mechanisms. *(He retreats into the fog when he feels threatened and thinks all are in the fog, but he is the only one concerned about it. He believes McMurphy is trying to drag the patients out of the fog where they will be easy prey. He correlates the fog with his experience in WWII, when the soldiers fogged in the airfield for protection. Remembering how easy it was to get lost in the real fog, he now tries not to get too deeply immersed in his mental fog because he does not want to be sent for more Electro-Shock treatments. As his anxiety and his concern for McMurphy increase, he resigns himself to his fate, allows the fog to overtake him, and learns to be quiet and inconspicuous. At one point, he imagines himself as part of a picture of mountains, where he vicariously enjoys fishing. pp. 104, 112–118)*

2. Examine McMurphy's actions following his prior conflict with Nurse Ratched over ward policies. Note the foreshadowing of the control panel. *(At first he is mannerly, laughs at the nurses and black aides, and refuses to lose his temper. He becomes angry and loses control at a Group Meeting when he wants to change the cleaning schedule and arrange for the men to watch the World Series on television. Nurse Ratched refuses, and McMurphy asks for a vote. With the exception of Cheswick, the Acutes say nothing because they feel it is futile to try and are afraid Ratched will make things worse for them. McMurphy becomes angry at their apathy and begins to win so much money from them that they refuse to play blackjack with him. McMurphy suggests escaping by throwing something through the windows. He realizes the only thing big enough is the control panel, which weighs about 400 pounds. Although McMurphy is unable to move the panel, this event foreshadows the day Chief Bromden will do so and escape. pp. 104–111)*

3. Discuss the dynamics of the Group Meeting. Analyze what the meeting reveals about Billy Bibbit and its effect on Bromden. *(Nurse Ratched initially intends to discuss whether or not McMurphy belongs on the ward because he is upsetting the patients. As the meeting begins, Nurse Ratched probes into the reasons Billy Bibbit stutters. He tells the group he stuttered over the word "Mama," the first word he said. His stuttering became so severe when he attempted to ask a girl to marry him that she laughed. Billy's stuttering symbolizes the control his mother exerts and her refusal to allow him to grow up and mature. He remains "Mama's little boy" and is unable to function in a normal world. Ratched destroys Billy's dignity, and he leaves. Bromden compares Billy to a prisoner. Colonel Matterson rambles incoherently, yet Bromden understands what he is saying. Bromden wants to help the patients, but doesn't know how. He is terrified and begins to hallucinate, feeling that he and the others are floating away in the fog. He feels dead, i.e., lost in the fog, unable to move, but without any pain. Memories of his childhood filter through his mind. pp. 118–123)*

4. Examine the escalation of the conflict between McMurphy and Ratched. Note the impact on Bromden. *(When McMurphy asks for another vote to watch the World Series, Nurse Ratched alludes to the possibility of moving him to another ward. Scanlon and Cheswick speak up in McMurphy's defense, and she allows the vote. All twenty Acutes vote for McMurphy, a sign that they are voting against Ratched. She refuses to concede, based on the lack of a true majority because none of the Chronics vote. The power struggle gets intense as McMurphy becomes irate and demands the right to speak to the Chronics, and Ratched asks Dr. Spivey to note his agitation. Ratched declares the meeting adjourned when none of the Chronics respond, but Bromden raises his hand, asserting himself for the first time. This is the turning point for Bromden as he demonstrates his power to think and choose for himself. Ratched refuses to accept his vote, saying the meeting was closed. She is obviously upset as she returns to the Nurses' Station. McMurphy turns on the TV, Nurse Ratched turns off the power, and he sits watching the blank TV screen as if nothing has happened. The other patients join him in a silent protest as Ratched screams at them about discipline. pp. 123–128)*

5. **Prediction:** Will McMurphy succeed in uniting the patients against Nurse Ratched?

Supplementary Activities

1. Assign students to act the roles of Nurse Ratched, McMurphy, and Billy Bibbit and have the class stage the Group Meeting.

2. Have students write a report of the Group Meeting from Dr. Spivey's point of view.

3. **Similes**—it [the screen] would dice him like an eggplant (p. 109); [horn] sounded like a goose honking (p. 116); faces blow past in the fog like confetti (p. 122) **Metaphor**—mental ward: Ol' Mother Ratched's Therapeutic Nursery (p. 107)

Part Two, pp. 129–151

The staff discusses what to do with McMurphy. Nurse Ratched chooses to keep him on her ward where she can control him. McMurphy becomes more aggressive in his taunting of Nurse Ratched, and the patients begin to exhibit bravery and self-respect. However, McMurphy soon becomes submissive after realizing his actions could possibly keep him in the hospital indefinitely.

Vocabulary
*arch type (134)
schizophrenic (135)
latent (135)
Oedipal (135)
blowhard (136)
silage (141)
impound (146)
hydrocephalus (149)
lymph (149)
*spelling in novel

Discussion Questions

1. Discuss the aftermath of the patients' silent protest. *(Patients and staff members now know that Nurse Ratched can lose control, and all watch her to see what she does next. She remains motionless at the Nurses' Station. Bromden thinks rationally and believes there is no more fog. He is afraid everyone knows he can hear, so he retreats behind his façade of deafness. Ratched calls a staff meeting to discuss McMurphy. For the next week, McMurphy continues to harass Nurse Ratched, even after she assigns him to latrine duty. The men continue their silent protest by lining up in front of the silent TV each afternoon when it is time for the World Series game. McMurphy entertains them. The patients become more assertive in the Group Meetings. Throughout section)*

2. Analyze the significance of what Bromden "sees" and must clean up in the staff room. Correlate his images with the discussion he overhears regarding McMurphy. *(He sees green, bitter light seeping out the peephole of the staff room and recalls the terrible "poisons" he has to clean up after the meetings. Because everyone assumes he is deaf, he is often in the room and overhears the staff discussing the patients. He has hallucinated about seeing the patient, nude and vulnerable, as the doctors and nurses speak derogatorily about him. Bromden compares their venomous words to poisons and acids strong enough to destroy any man. Although Ratched is suspicious after Bromden's affirmative vote in the Group Meeting, she allows him to remain in the room while they discuss McMurphy. pp. 131–132)*

3. Discuss the staff meeting regarding McMurphy and analyze the irony of their diagnosis of him. Note the foreshadowing of McMurphy's martyrdom. *(The staff doctor tells the others they are not dealing with an ordinary man. The residents, attempting to please Nurse Ratched, speak of him as a disturbing influence and a dangerous man. One resident suggests that his actions could be those of a sane, shrewd con-man rather than one who is mentally ill. Still trying to please Ratched, another resident diagnoses him as a Potential Assaultive patterned after Napoleon, Genghis Khan, and Attila the Hun, and another mimics the nurse's comments about McMurphy being disturbed. Conflict erupts among the residents. The option of placing McMurphy on the Disturbed Ward for observation is discussed. Ratched disagrees with the idea, remarking that he must not become a martyr to the other men and that they must not view him as extraordinary. She intends to keep him on her ward and break his will, saying she has all the time she needs because he is committed. Irony: The resident's diagnosis that McMurphy is sane is based on an incorrect assumption, i.e., his shrewdness rather than his ability to make a rational choice proves his sanity. Ratched's conclusion that McMurphy is ordinary is based on her opinion that he exhibits the behavior of "ordinary" insanity, such as Cheswick. In reality, he is truly ordinary because he is, in fact, sane. pp. 132–136)*

4. Examine the changes in Chief Bromden. *(He looks in the mirror and reflects on his inability to be who he really is and wonders how McMurphy can be what he is. He observes things about McMurphy other than his outward persona, e.g., his artistic abilities and his sensitivity. For the first time in years, Bromden sees people without the foggy outline, he thinks clearly, and he lives in a world of reality rather than fantasy. He looks out the window on a clear night and realizes the hospital is out in the country. He observes and enjoys the outside world. pp. 140–143)*

5. Discuss why McMurphy becomes submissive to Nurse Ratched and the effect this has on the other patients. *(During an outing to the swimming pool, McMurphy tells the lifeguard how much better it is to be in the mental hospital than to be on the work farm. The lifeguard explains the difference: a jail sentence has a release date, but being committed to a mental hospital means an indefinite stay. He tells McMurphy that he was committed to the institution after being picked up for drunk and disorderly and has remained for almost nine years. McMurphy realizes that Nurse Ratched is confident and unruffled by his antics because she can keep him in the institution indefinitely. He realizes he made a mistake by faking insanity to escape the prison work farm, because he only had four months left to complete his prison sentence. McMurphy becomes cooperative and submissive because he wants to be released. He changes his tactics, e.g., cleans and polishes the latrine, ignores Cheswick's plea for verbal support, and no longer stands up for the other patients. Bromden becomes afraid and begins to hallucinate again. The others at first think McMurphy is biding his time, but Bromden knows what he is doing and thinks it is wise. All finally understand that they have lost their "defender." On the next trip to the swimming pool, Cheswick drowns, with the inference that he commits suicide. pp. 146–151)*

Supplementary Activities

1. Working with a partner, have students write a short essay in which they address one of the following: (a) McMurphy is an ordinary man because... or (b) McMurphy is an extraordinary man because....

2. **Similes**—whack...sounds like a gavel (p. 136); guys heaped in long white rows like snowbanks (p. 141) **Metaphor/Allusion**—This man [McMurphy]: Napoleon, Genghis Khan, Attila the Hun (p. 134)

pp. 152–173

The mood in the ward changes when McMurphy ceases to protest. McMurphy shows signs of stress and learns about Electro-Shock Therapy and lobotomy. The patients reveal that, unlike McMurphy, they are all in the mental hospital voluntarily and can leave any time they choose. This revelation infuriates McMurphy, and he reaches a turning point, choosing again to rebel against Nurse Ratched's control.

Vocabulary
kneading (153)
schematic (157)
curtail (158)
nemesis (158)
punitive (163)
lobotomy (163)
aplomb (163)
vogue (164)
lucid (165)
spoor (169)
circumvent (171)

Discussion Questions

1. Correlate Sefelt's seizure with Nurse Ratched's manipulative power over the patients. Note the symbolism of Sefelt's position on the floor. *(When Sefelt has an epileptic seizure because he refuses to take his medication, Nurse Ratched subtly warns the other Acutes about refusing their medication. She acts solicitous, but the patients sense undertones of hostility. It is obvious she has resumed control, and the ward again operates on a mechanical timetable in which no one protests her decisions. Sefelt is stretched out with hands "nailed" out to each side, palms up, just as patients receiving EST on the cross-like table, symbolizing martyrdom on a cross. pp. 152–156)*

2. Discuss Harding's wife, Vera, and examine the implications of her visit. *(When she comes to visit, Harding doesn't make a move toward her and knows everyone is watching. He introduces her to McMurphy as his "Nemesis." His hands shake, and he hides his hands when he realizes Vera and McMurphy are watching him "talk" with them. Vera criticizes and humiliates her husband, and they quarrel. She flaunts her sexuality and sprinkles her conversation with sexual innuendoes. She implies infidelity and/or homosexuality when she refers to his friends who visit her as having long hair and limp little wrists. pp. 157–159)*

3. Analyze the significance of McMurphy's actions following Vera's visit. Discuss the possible meanings of his dreams. *(As he looks down at Sefelt, McMurphy's face takes on a haggard, puzzled look. He apologizes to the other patients for his previous outburst and acknowledges he has been having bad dreams in which he sees nothing but faces. Possible meaning of McMurphy's dreams: He sees the faces of the men who have come to believe in and rely on him to escape their mental torment. He struggles with the possible repercussions of his future actions—for him personally and for the other men. pp. 155, 160–161)*

4. Discuss the information Harding gives McMurphy about Electro-Shock Therapy and lobotomies. Analyze the symbolism of the lobotomy. Note Harding's sarcasm and analyze the metaphor comparing EST to "Brain Burning." *(While waiting for a routine chest X-ray, McMurphy sees patients being wheeled in and out of the EST room. Harding tells McMurphy about the "Shock Shop" where the patient is strapped to a table before undergoing EST. The patient always*

tries to avoid getting another treatment because it changes him, e.g., causes him to forget things. Their discussion of EST and lobotomies, a procedure in which portions of the brain are cut away, foreshadows what will happen to McMurphy. Symbolism: Harding refers to a lobotomy as frontal-lobe castration, symbolizing Ratched's use of physical mutilation if mental emasculation fails to work. Sarcasm: Harding tells McMurphy everything done at the hospital is "for the patient's good," but then alludes to the staff's sadism, including Ratched's use of EST for punishment. Harding remarks that electricity is at least more humane than a hammer. Metaphor: Harding compares EST to "Brain Burning" because a patient loses brain cells each time the electricity goes through his brain, i.e., cells are burned out. pp. 162–165)

5. Analyze the conversation between McMurphy and the others about Nurse Ratched. Note the foreshadowing about McMurphy. *(Harding and most of the patients agree that Nurse Ratched is the root of the trouble at the institution, but McMurphy believes something bigger than Ratched creates the mess. Bromden associates this statement with his belief about the Combine, both the one at the hospital and the one that exists nation-wide. McMurphy classifies Ratched as a bitter, icy-hearted old woman. The conversation switches to McMurphy's rationale for changing his tactics with Ratched. He tells the others he must look out for himself because he doesn't want to remain at the institution any longer than he has to. He acknowledges feeling that the others have conned him into speaking up for them. Harding reveals that most of the men on the ward are not committed and can leave when they wish. Billy blurts out that they don't have the courage to leave and begins to cry hysterically. The others stare at McMurphy, leaving him puzzled and struggling for answers. Foreshadowing: McMurphy refers to the patients coming to him like he was their savior. pp. 165–168)*

6. Discuss the resumption of hostilities between McMurphy and Ratched. Note that this is the turning point of the plot. *(As they return from the building that houses the EST, Bromden realizes that McMurphy is his usual mischievous self. During a Group Meeting, Ratched manipulates the patients as usual and concludes the meeting by announcing punishment for the ward concerning their prior house duties—she is taking away their privilege of using the tub room for their card games. The men hopefully turn toward McMurphy, who grins, tips his hat, and starts toward the Nurses' Station. He asks for his cigarettes, then punches his hand through the glass, shattering it. Ratched is frightened and realizes he has foiled her plan of complete control. In the turning point, McMurphy once again establishes his leadership of the patients and the ward. pp. 169–173)*

7. **Prediction:** Who will win in the conflict between McMurphy and Ratched? How?

Supplementary Activities

1. Divide the class in half. Have one group research electroshock therapy, a.k.a. electroconvulsive therapy, while the other group researches the method and use of the lobotomy. Students will then prepare an oral report and participate in a class discussion.

2. **Similes**—fingernails are red as drops of blood (p. 157); ...it's as if the jolt sets off a wild carnival wheel of images (p. 164) **Metaphors**—Electro-Shock Therapy: trip to the moon, Brain Burning (pp. 162, 163)

Part Three, pp. 174–190

Other Acutes follow McMurphy's lead and become more aggressive. McMurphy gets approval from Dr. Spivey for a fishing trip. Chief Bromden reveals incidents from his childhood.

Vocabulary
hovel (180)
fraternize (180)
squalor (180)
indigents (189)

Discussion Questions

1. Examine changes in the ward following McMurphy's shattering of the window at the Nurses' Station. Note changes in Nurse Ratched. Why doesn't she simply recommend McMurphy's release and rid herself of the problem? *(McMurphy has his way for a long while. Ratched bides her time until she comes up with another idea and does not intend to recommend his release. They treat each other politely, while the other Acutes become more aggressive. McMurphy involves himself with everything on the ward. He jokes with the men and requests an Accompanied Pass. After Ratched denies his request, he breaks the window again, and Scanlon accidentally breaks it a third time. Ratched begins showing signs of strain. McMurphy writes more notes for her to find in the latrine, writes long, outlandish tales about himself in the log book, and often sleeps until 8:00 a.m. Dr. Spivey becomes more assertive and supports McMurphy in improving the lives of the men, e.g., he organizes a basketball team. McMurphy finally receives permission from the staff for an Accompanied Pass to take the men fishing. Answers will vary. pp. 174–177)*

2. Discuss McMurphy's plans for the fishing trip and his ensuing battle of wills with Nurse Ratched. *(His request lists two "sweet old aunts," as chaperones who are actually prostitutes that McMurphy is acquainted with. He tells the men about the deep-sea fishing trip and begins to sign them up for $10.00 each. Ratched counteracts by posting a series of clippings about wrecked boats and sudden storms. The battle of wills continues, with McMurphy encouraging the men and Ratched discouraging them. Her influence creates problems for McMurphy, and he finds it difficult to get enough men to pay for the boat. pp. 177–178)*

3. Analyze Bromden's statement, "…it wasn't me that started acting deaf; it was people that first started acting like I was too dumb to hear or see or say anything at all" (p. 178). Discuss similar situations you have experienced or observed. *(He is thinking about the years of pretending to be deaf and wondering if he can ever act any other way. People began to act like he was deaf and mute long before he came to the hospital. He first noticed it when he was about ten. Visitors were speaking derogatorily about the Indian village and people, and he attempted to tell them the truth. They did not look at him or act as if they heard him. Other incidents include people in grade school who quit listening to what he said, and anyone in the Army with more stripes than he ignored him. Bromden realizes this is the first time in a long time he has been able to remember much about his childhood. This marks a turning point for him. Answers will vary. pp. 178–182)*

4. Examine the interaction between McMurphy and Bromden and what this reveals about both of them. *(Geever is scraping Bromden's chewing gum from beneath his bed. McMurphy awakens and Geever explains what he is doing and why. McMurphy begins to laugh and sing about the chewing gum losing its flavor overnight. At first Bromden thinks he is laughing at him, but begins to see the humor and starts to chuckle. McMurphy gives him a pack of gum. For the first time Bromden speaks, saying "Thank you." He tries to laugh, but it is more like crying, and he can't verbalize his feelings. McMurphy begins to talk about a time he was ignored so he hushed and listened until the last day working in the field, when he repeated everything he had heard. Bromden begins to talk, telling McMurphy about his parents and his father's alcoholism and warning him that the Combine will get him. Thinking McMurphy has gone to sleep, Bromden wants to touch*

him just because "he is who he is." McMurphy again begins to talk and discovers that Bromden wants to go on the fishing trip but doesn't have the money. He offers to pay Bromden's $10.00 if he will prove he can lift the control panel and then offers to help Bromden become "big" again. This foreshadows Bromden's lifting the panel and escaping. pp. 183–190)

5. Discuss what Bromden reveals to McMurphy and examine how earlier events shaped his future. *(Bromden believes McMurphy to be bigger and tougher than he is. When McMurphy tells him that he stands a head taller than any man on the ward, Bromden tells him that he used to be big but is now half the size of McMurphy. Bromden then tells McMurphy that his father was very big when Bromden was a child but that his mother got twice his size. As he relates the story of his childhood, McMurphy realizes that Bromden's mother's huge size is figurative, not literal. Bromden's father, who was an Indian chief, took the last name of his wife, who was white. Bromden blames his mother and the Combine, i.e., his own people and the government, for destroying his father. The government wanted to take everything from him, and he gave up because his wife made him too small to fight anymore. He began to drink excessively, which eventually led to his death. Bromden's belief that he is small is indicative of his low self-esteem and reflects his intimidation and fear that the Combine will also destroy him. pp. 186–188)*

6. **Prediction:** Will McMurphy succeed in taking the men fishing?

Supplementary Activities

1. Working in small groups, have students prepare a series of five Public Service Announcements (PSA) for radio, TV, or the newspaper encouraging parents or guardians to listen to their children. Each PSA should be one minute long. If prepared for the newspaper, the PSA should include a visual aid; for TV, a staged script.

2. **Similes**—Martini picked it [the ball] off the floor like a dead bird (p. 177); scissors open like jaws (p. 183); laugh…like a pullet trying to crow (p. 185) **Metaphors**—man's head: red rubber ball (p. 179); government: Combine (p. 187)

pp. 191–218

Candy, a prostitute, and Dr. Spivey act as chaperones for the patients' fishing trip. McMurphy defies the boat's owner in order to take the men fishing.

Vocabulary
keelhaul (192)
wistful (192)
turret (204)
cormorants (210)

Discussion Questions

1. Discuss the initial phases of the fishing trip. Analyze public reaction to the patients. Discuss whether or not you think reactions to mental illness have changed during the last 40 years. *(McMurphy signs up Bromden as the ninth man. George Sorensen, who worked for 25 years on Chinook trollers, wants to go but is afraid of the germs. McMurphy manipulates him into going by implying that he is scared of the ocean and by telling him that he will be the captain. Candy is the only "chaperone" who comes, and ten men cannot fit into one car. McMurphy talks Dr. Spivey into going and taking his car, foiling Nurse Ratched's "victory." The patients are uneasy and almost return to the safety of the hospital. The service station attendants suspiciously eye the patients and are reluctant to help them. The men feel even worse after Dr. Spivey lies, saying the men are a work crew. McMurphy foils the attendant's attempts to exploit the patients by telling them that they are from the criminally insane ward and are entitled to a*

discount because they are on a government-authorized excursion. He threatens one of them, then tells him to send the bill for the gas to the hospital. McMurphy's actions inspire the other patients to act with bravado and courage during the drive to the ocean. Answers will vary. pp. 191–203)

2. Examine McMurphy's actions at the dock and discuss the fishing expedition. Note changes in the patients. *(The boat's captain refuses to take the group out without a signed waiver clearing him with the authorities. He makes disparaging remarks about the patients, and men on the dock insult Candy. McMurphy and the captain argue, and McMurphy suggests making a phone call to clear things up. The patients lose their bravado as the two men go up to the bait shack. While the captain is on the phone, McMurphy prompts the group to get into the boat, and Sorensen guides it away from shore and eventually into the open sea. McMurphy stands back and laughs as the men reel in fish, and Bromden realizes laughter is his defense against the world. Changes: all learn to laugh again; Bromden becomes an integral part of the group; all, including Dr. Spivey, work together; Billy Bibbit displays courage; Sorensen regains a sense of worth by his expertise as captain; McMurphy steps back and allows others to be the heroes. pp. 204–214)*

3. Analyze the significance of the men's return to the dock and to the hospital. *(The captain, policemen, and loafers come charging down the steps. Dr. Spivey takes the initiative by telling the policemen they do not have jurisdiction over the patients, and they will have to take the matter up with a federal agency. He threatens the captain with an investigation into why there are not enough life jackets for everyone. McMurphy and the captain argue and scuffle but go off together to get beer. Instead of insulting Candy, the loafers discuss the size of Spivey's halibut and ask Sorensen where he learned his expertise, then all share a beer together before the group leaves. The patients are no longer "weak-knees" who will take insults. With McMurphy's help, Billy arranges for a date with Candy. Bromden is learning to enjoy life again. When they return to the hospital, everyone except McMurphy is excited. Bromden has noticed McMurphy's exhausted, strained expression throughout the entire day. pp. 214–218)*

Supplementary Activities

1. Have students choose one of the participants in the fishing expedition and write a diary entry about his or her day on the ocean.

2. **Similes**—arms rustled...like paper wings (p. 191); [sea] like a field of glass and chrome (p. 213) **Metaphors**—hospital patients: cracked pots of mankind, service station attendants: pigeons (p. 202) **Allusions**—Old Man of the Sea: *The Old Man and the Sea* (p. 194); Hitler (p. 202)

Part Four, pp. 219–241

Nurse Ratched causes the patients to question McMurphy's motives. McMurphy and Bromden fight the black aides in defense of Sorensen and are sent to the Disturbed Ward, where they receive Electro-Shock Therapy.

Vocabulary
philanthropy (222)
capitalistic (223)
chicanery (223)
effrontery (223)

Discussion Questions

1. Discuss Nurse Ratched's next maneuver and its effect on the men. Note the irony of her actions. *(The day after the fishing trip, she begins to imply that McMurphy's dealings with the men are always for his benefit and hints at his past reputation as a con-man. She posts a statement of each patient's financial status in the past few months, showing a steady drain from all the Acutes' funds except McMurphy's, which shows a steady increase. Patients start to*

joke with him about taking them down. He doesn't deny it and brags about gaining financial independence if he stays in the hospital for one year. The patients begin to question his motives. Ratched's first ploy to undermine him in a Group Meeting fails because he counteracts her, so she makes sure he is absent from the next meeting. She gives the men a "chance" to discuss McMurphy. The men tell funny stories about him and concede that he is a great guy. She maneuvers the conversation to questions about his actions and makes the statement that he is "crazy like a fox." After Billy Bibbit defends him, she begins to enumerate McMurphy's "gifts" to the patients and the list of his bets, pointing out that he has won almost $300 from the men. As the men discuss McMurphy after the meeting, Harding speaks of his capitalistic talent and his trickery. Only two men, Bibbit and Bromden, continue to believe in him, but Bibbit is swayed when McMurphy suggests that he send money to Candy. Even Bromden questions McMurphy when he detects his motive for having him lift the control panel. Irony: Ratched accuses McMurphy of manipulating the men when she is the one who manipulates. McMurphy is always honest about his schemes. pp. 219–224)

2. Discuss changes in Bromden's feelings toward McMurphy. Note the irony of their conversation about "winning." *(McMurphy reminds him of their deal, i.e., he would pay Bromden's $10.00 for the fishing trip if he would try to lift the control panel. Bromden is able to move the panel six inches off the floor. When McMurphy begins to talk about strength and the panel, Bromden thinks he is going to prove he doesn't do everything for money by telling the men how he helped Bromden get his size back. However, McMurphy doesn't mention Bromden, but instead maneuvers the talk and "reluctantly" takes five-to-one bets from the others that no one can lift the panel. Bromden keeps hoping McMurphy will change his mind, but the next day he has Bromden lift the panel. He feels he has helped McMurphy cheat the others and runs out of the room. He refuses the $5.00 McMurphy offers him, and in their ensuing conversation, Bromden tells him "You're always…winning things!" Irony: McMurphy's response about winning indicates that he knows he is losing. He is winning money, but is destined to lose his life. pp. 225–227)*

3. Examine the causes and effects in this section. Note the men's premonition about what is going to happen, why it has to happen, and why they've been wrong about McMurphy. *(Cause: the patients' fishing trip. Effect: Nurse Ratched's orders for all to take a special shower. Cause: black aides attempt to force Sorensen to allow them to "cleanse" him. Effect: He refuses. Cause: Sorensen becomes hysterical after aides taunt him. Effect: McMurphy intervenes. Cause: McMurphy calls Washington, the aide, derogatory names. Effect: Washington ignores him. Cause: McMurphy is forced to initiate the confrontation. Effect: He and Washington fight. Cause: One of the other aides comes to Washington's defense. Effect: Bromden joins McMurphy in the fray. Cause: The smallest aide goes for help. Effect: Nurse Ratched and aides from the Disturbed Ward strap and cuff McMurphy and Bromden. Cause: McMurphy and Bromden are subdued. Effect: They are taken to the Disturbed Ward. pp. 227–232)*

4. Discuss the atmosphere of the Disturbed Ward and examine the significance of the events while McMurphy and Bromden are there. *(Fear pervades the ward. Many of the men are berserk and out of control. As the nurse gently tends to McMurphy's wounds, she refers to Ratched being a retired Army nurse and tells the two men that other nurses are opposed to her control and treatment of her patients. She would like to keep them on her ward but cannot do so. Bromden wants to stand tall, reflecting his emergence from feelings of insignificance, yet he still wants to shrink away from Ratched. Images and sounds of fear emerge from the EST room. When it is McMurphy and Bromden's turn to enter the room, Bromden feels himself slipping from reality and imagining he is in an air raid. McMurphy offers to go first and jokes with the technicians. During Bromden's treatment, he retreats into childhood memories of his father. He wills himself not to retreat into the fog again and quickly emerges from the effects of the treatment. He now knows he has them beat, i.e., he will regain full sanity. pp. 232–241)*

5. Analyze the meaning of the statement, "…in the corners and under the Ping-pong table there's things crouched gnashing their teeth that the doctors and nurses can't see and the aides can't kill with disinfectant" (p. 232). *(Answers will vary. Suggestions: This symbolizes the fear, oppression, and derangement that lurk everywhere. In their disturbed state, the men see things that aren't there but that seem real and frightening to them. No amount of scrubbing can eliminate these "things" because they exist in the minds of the patients.)*

6. Analyze Ratched's tactics to reduce McMurphy to the level of her other patients and his response to her. *(She talks to him in a conciliatory voice about his childish tantrum and tries to shame him into admitting he was wrong by subtly threatening shock therapy. She tells him the men in the Group Meeting agree with the staff that shock treatment might be beneficial unless he realizes his mistakes. He compares her to the Chinese Communists when he was a prisoner of war, refuses to concede, and asks where the table is. She orders EST for him. pp. 235–236)*

7. Discuss the significance of Bromden's memories during his EST. Note especially the symbolism of his grandmother's rhyme. *(Memories of his childhood intermingle with irrational thoughts. He recalls his childhood and the conflict of being half-Indian and half-white. His father taught him Indian traditions, but his mother insisted their family was civilized and white. When his father married Mary Louise Bromden, he took her last name because she refused to take his. After his Indian grandmother died and was buried, he helped his father dig up her body and hang her in a pine tree according to Indian custom. His grandmother taught him a game accompanied by the rhyme, "One flew east, one flew west, one flew over the cuckoo's nest…O-U-T spells out…" Recalling this gives him the impetus to escape some day, figuratively and literally. pp. 238–241)*

Supplementary Activities

1. Have students recall and recite some childhood rhymes. Brainstorm with them concerning whether or not they think the rhymes have an implied meaning.

2. **Similes**—[McMurphy] crazy like a fox (p. 221); alarm sounds like a gigantic pencil-sharpener (p. 234) **Metaphors**—McMurphy: giant (p. 224); nurse's fingers: pink birthday candles (p. 233) **Personification**—The metal door looks out with its rivet eyes (p. 236).

pp. 242–259

McMurphy receives three more rounds of EST. After returning to the ward, he bribes the night aide, Mr. Turkle, to arrange for Candy's visit to the ward. Candy and Sandra arrive, bringing alcohol with them. The patients, for the first time, loosen up and act "normal." They all get drunk, and Candy spends the night with Billy. The patients try to convince McMurphy to escape, but he insists he needs to sleep first. The black aides arrive the next morning to find all of the men asleep in various spots around the ward.

Vocabulary
provocative (248)
chastising (258)

Discussion Questions

1. Discuss the effects of EST on Bromden and McMurphy and analyze why Ratched has McMurphy returned to the ward. *(Bromden recovers in less than a day, compared to his previous two-week recovery times. When he emerges, he feels as if he has just come from a deep dive after being underwater for a hundred years. This is the last treatment he ever receives. When he returns to the ward, the men treat him as a hero, and Bromden relishes their*

respect. *McMurphy receives three more treatments after refusing to concur with Ratched's wishes. Although he insists the treatments aren't hurting him, his jaw goes taut, his face drains of color, and he looks thin and scared before each treatment. The men on the ward laugh at Ratched over an incident with McMurphy, and she realizes he is strengthening in their eyes. She has him returned to the ward because she thinks he will return from EST in a shock stupor and wants to make him look weak and vulnerable. However, he returns with the bravado of a boxer, announces the champ is back, and resumes his pranks. pp. 242–244)*

2. Discuss the men's plan for McMurphy and why it doesn't succeed. *(They know Ratched will continue to send him for EST and plan to set a fire so he can escape when the firemen come. He reminds them that it is Saturday, the day Candy is coming for her date with Billy. p. 244)*

3. Discuss the events that transpire during the men's Saturday night party and what this reveals about the men. *(McMurphy continues to prepare and encourage Billy for his night with Candy. McMurphy arranges with Mr. Turkle, the night aide, to get Candy into the hospital, enticing him with the possibility of liquor and sex. Candy arrives after 2:00 a.m., bringing Sandra and some wine. A party atmosphere fills the ward as the men laugh, joke, and drink the wine. They enter the Nurses' Station and read the patients' files. Bromden gets drunk and runs, laughs, carries on with the women in the center of the Combine's most powerful stronghold, an indication to him that the Combine isn't all powerful. Harding takes the initiative in preventing the supervisor from discovering all of them in the latrine and in suggesting a plan that will allow McMurphy to escape and Turkle to keep his job, as well as keep the rest of them out of trouble. McMurphy seems to agree to the escape plan but is still there the next morning. Billy and Candy spend the night together, and everyone is still asleep when the black aides arrive at 6:30 a.m. pp. 248–259)*

4. Discuss the information revealed about Billy Bibbit and analyze the effect his relationship with his mother has on him. *(Bromden's information about Billy's mother explains his immaturity and insecurity: she works as a receptionist in the hospital lobby, she and Nurse Ratched are close friends, and she expects Billy to kiss her goodbye when the group leaves for an activity. Bromden overhears an earlier conversation in which Billy, as he lies on the grass with his head in his mother's lap, tells her of his desire to find a wife and go to college. When he mentions his age, his mother denies looking old enough to have a middle-aged son. Her domination and possessiveness of him ultimately lead to his suicide because he cannot face the consequences when she learns of his night with Candy. pp. 246–247)*

5. Analyze the symbolism of Fredrickson's sprinkling pills over Sefelt and Sandra like "crumbling clods into a grave." *(As they lie on the floor, he sprinkles the pills, then utters a mock prayer as if he is officiating at their funeral. He "prays" for Sefelt and Sandra, then asks God to keep the doors open for the rest of them because they are witnessing the "end." Fredrickson realizes this is the last "fling" for all of them and they are doomed to be "shot at dawn" by Nurse Ratched, who will tranquilize them into oblivion. Symbolically, this night marks the end of Ratched's control, McMurphy's freedom and soon his life, and the hospitalization of most of the Acutes. pp. 254–255, inference)*

6. Examine Harding and Bromden's conversation with McMurphy about escaping and analyze Harding's summation of reasons the men suffer from mental illnesses. *(Harding believes the men are not quite ready to leave. He says he plans to leave soon, but wants to walk out properly to prove he is able to do it that way. Bromden doesn't yet know where he wants to go and feels he should stay for a few weeks after McMurphy leaves to keep things from sliding back. Harding believes the others are still sick in many ways but believes they can be well some day. He attributes mental illness to guilt, shame, fear, and self-belittlement. He tells McMurphy that "they," the mentally ill, drive strong people down the road to insanity. pp. 256–259)*

7. Why doesn't McMurphy escape when given the opportunity? *(Answers will vary. Suggestion: McMurphy is willing to sacrifice himself for the other patients' happiness and "freedom." He is determined to beat Nurse Ratched, and the only way he can win is to stay for the final confrontation. McMurphy appears strong on the outside, but he is growing tired of the daily battles. He may be resigning himself to the fact that he will never escape his own conscience and feelings of insecurity.)*

8. **Prediction:** What will happen to McMurphy? to Nurse Ratched? to the other patients?

Supplementary Activities

1. Find and read aloud the poem "She Walks in Beauty" (see the allusion on page 248 of the novel) by Lord Byron. Have students work with a partner and (a) write a poem (b) write lyrics to a song or (c) create a picture collage contrasting the lady in Byron's poem with Candy.

2. **Similes**—Their faces lighted up as if they were looking into the glare of a sideshow platform (p. 243); Her smile broke like glass (p. 245) **Metaphor/Allusion**—Chief Bromden: Goliath (p. 250) **Allusion**—masked man with silver bullet—the Lone Ranger (p. 258)

pp. 260–272

Upon her arrival on the ward, Nurse Ratched discovers the sleeping patients. Determined to regain her authority, she attempts to turn the patients against McMurphy. When no one will accept blame for the party, she provokes Billy Bibbit, threatening to tell his mother about his behavior with Candy. Unable to face his mother, Billy commits suicide. After Nurse Ratched blames McMurphy for Billy's death, he attacks her, seriously injuring her. She arranges for him to undergo a lobotomy. As a result, McMurphy is left incapacitated and unresponsive. Bromden, knowing McMurphy wouldn't want to live this way, suffocates his comatose friend, throws the control panel through the window, and escapes.

Vocabulary
shellacked (261)
atrocities (262)
discretion (264)
contemptuous (265)
skittered (268)
syndicate (272)

Discussion Questions

1. Discuss the aftermath of the party and examine references to fate. *(Everyone is gathered in the day room. Those involved wait in quiet wonder; those not involved are incredulous. Harding remains rational. McMurphy looks sick and very tired, but still refuses to try to escape. Turkle "resigns" and leaves with Candy. All wait for Nurse Ratched's wrath. Fate: In retrospect, Bromden rationalizes that the events in the denouement were bound to be and were destined to happen some time, some way. Ratched would have discovered what went on and reacted the same way. Billy would have done what he did, and McMurphy would have returned because he would not have allowed Ratched to win. Bromden reflects that McMurphy signed on for the whole game and there was not any way to avoid his destiny. This sets the stage for the denouement of the novel. pp. 260–261)*

2. Analyze the key points in Ratched's effect on Billy Bibbit. Note the irony of the accusations she directs toward McMurphy. *(She shames Billy for being with "a woman like this" and says the news will make his mother ill when she tells her. Billy has been pleased and satisfied until this, but then becomes agitated and begs her not to tell. He falls to the floor in a panic and begins to blame the others, especially Candy, McMurphy, and Harding. Ratched gives him the "silent treatment," then begins to treat him like a child, e.g., embraces him, assures him no one will harm*

him, calls him a "poor little boy." She figuratively emasculates him in front of the others. After she puts him in the doctor's office to wait, he commits suicide by cutting his throat. Irony: she accuses McMurphy of playing with human lives as if he thinks he is God and blames Cheswick and Billy's deaths on him. It is actually she who drives the men to suicide by the same actions of which she now accuses McMurphy. She is the one who attempts to "play God" through manipulation and control. pp. 263–265)

3. Examine McMurphy's final confrontation with Nurse Ratched and analyze the symbolism of the attack. *(This is his "final round." Ratched blames McMurphy for Billy's suicide. Bromden realizes what he is about to do but also acknowledges that it is McMurphy's destiny to sacrifice himself for them, and no one can stop him. The patients' need provides the momentum and inspiration for his actions: continuing when he is exhausted, smiling and defying EST, and attacking Nurse Ratched. McMurphy jumps on Nurse Ratched and rips her uniform, thus exposing her both literally and figuratively. Before he is subdued, he chokes her, leaving her unable to speak, symbolical of the loss of a vital human quality. This compares with Bromden, who figuratively lost his voice. He regains not only his voice but also his humanity. McMurphy's cry just before he is restrained is a mixture of fear, hate, surrender, and defiance such as a hunted animal who no longer cares about anything but himself and his dying. This cry symbolizes McMurphy's final submission to his sacrificial "death." pp. 266–267)*

4. Discuss the denouement and whether you think McMurphy wins or loses. *(Nurse Ratched returns to the ward a week after the attack, bruised, unable to speak, and fearful. She cannot regain her control of the men. Several Acutes, including Harding, sign themselves out of the hospital and most of the others transfer to another ward, leaving only Bromden, Martini, and Scanlon. Bromden stays because he senses that Nurse Ratched has one last play. Three weeks later, McMurphy returns, almost unrecognizable after undergoing a lobotomy that leaves him one of the Chronic Vegetables. Patients walk by to stare at him. Bromden foils Ratched's plan of using McMurphy as an example of what can happen if a patient defies her by suffocating McMurphy with a pillow. Bromden then lifts the control panel, throws it through the window, and escapes. Through McMurphy's death, Nurse Ratched wins a victory, i.e., she destroys him, but McMurphy ultimately triumphs. His sacrificial death sets the others free, some literally and others figuratively, from Ratched's control. pp. 268–272)*

Supplementary Activities

1. Brainstorm with students and list emotions that are exhibited in this section, e.g., fear, love (sacrificial), apprehension, guilt, shame, anger. Have each student create a representation of one of these emotions as it is portrayed in the novel. Instruct students to use their own illustrations or pictures and words cut out from a magazine or newspaper.

2. **Similes**—wheelchairs parked…like empty rides in an amusement park (p. 260); [Billy] put his hand to his cheek like he'd been burned with acid (p. 264); The glass splashed…like a bright cold water baptizing the sleeping earth (pp. 271–272) **Metaphors**—Nurse Ratched: Angel of Mercy [sarcasm] (p. 262); Billy: Eloper (p. 262); McMurphy: boxer (inference, p. 265)

Post-reading Discussion Questions

Note: Responses to the following Discussion Questions will vary, but suggested answers are given where applicable. For items 1–5, have students present their graphic organizers and discuss them in groups

1. Use the Character Web on page 8 of this guide to characterize Randle Patrick McMurphy, Nurse Ratched, and Chief Bromden. *(Suggestion for Randle Patrick McMurphy—Feelings: self-confident, insolent, shocked; Demographics: Korean War veteran, former prisoner of war, con man, accused of statutory rape; Actions: dynamic, non-conformist, manipulative, sexually overt, self-sacrificial; Prized Possessions: deck of cards, whale-covered shorts.)*

2. Using the Character Chart on page 9 of this guide, complete the chart and discuss the instances in which each of these characters feels frustration, anger, fear, humiliation, relief, and hopelessness.

3. Using the Cause/Effect chart on page 10 of this guide, examine examples of cause and effect in the novel. In the space provided below the chart, write "McMurphy dies" in the Effect box and determine the causes. *(Examples of cause and effect in the novel—Cause: Billy Bibbit's domineering, stifling mother; Effect: Billy's immaturity and mental illness. Cause: Dale Harding's assertive, controlling wife; Effect: Harding's withdrawal into mental illness. Cause: Failure of adults to listen to Bromden, his father's alcoholism, and his mother's domination; Effect: Bromden's retreat into silence and mental illness. Cause: McMurphy is sentenced to work on the prison farm; Effect: he fakes mental illness to get away, etc. Causes of McMurphy's death—Nurse Ratched's determination to keep the mental patients under her control, Billy Bibbit's suicide, McMurphy's own inclination to sacrifice himself for others)*

4. Use the Foreshadowing Chart on page 11 of this guide to identify examples of foreshadowing throughout the novel. *(Nurse Ratched's reference to Mr. Taber's "fate": McMurphy's lobotomy [p. 29]; McMurphy's questions about moving the control panel: Bromden will someday move it [pp. 109, 189, 225]; Ratched's reference to McMurphy being under her control: he is committed and will be in the hospital indefinitely [p. 127]; Ratched's reference to McMurphy's being a martyr to the others: he becomes a martyr [p. 136]; Discussion about lobotomy: McMurphy will undergo a lobotomy [pp. 164–165, 243–244]; McMurphy's comment about "winning": he knows he will eventually lose [p. 227])*

5. Using the plot graph on page 12 of this guide, analyze the plot development. Discuss the instances in the novel when McMurphy and Bromden reach the turning point in their destiny. *(Characters: McMurphy, Nurse Ratched, Bromden, other patients; Setting: Oregon mental hospital, late 1950s; Problem: Ratched's reprehensible control of ward for mental patients; Beginning: McMurphy arrives as patient; Building Action: [1] He determines to obliterate the oppressive atmosphere of the ward. [2] He engages in numerous conflicts with Nurse Ratched. [3] He determines to submit to her when he learns she controls whether or not he is released. [4] Her actions cause him to change his mind and continue harassing her. [5] He attacks Washington in defense of Sorensen after their fishing trip. [6] Ratched orders EST for him. [7] Ratched becomes irate after the patients have a party. [8] Billy Bibbit commits suicide; Climax: McMurphy attacks Nurse Ratched; Resolution: Ratched orders a lobotomy for McMurphy. Most of the men leave the hospital or transfer to another ward. Bromden suffocates the comatose McMurphy and then escapes; Discussions will vary.)*

6. Analyze the roles of women in the novel. Note the irony of the way the women are portrayed. *(Most of the women in the book are portrayed as strong, domineering women who use their power over the men to mentally and emotionally emasculate them. Nurse Ratched represses her own sexuality yet probes into the sexuality of her patients' past. She manipulates the inmates and ultimately destroys their self-esteem. Bromden believes that his mother became progressively bigger as his father became smaller because she belittled him and controlled him. Billy Bibbit's mother controls him by treating him like a child and belittling his attempts to mature emotionally and sexually. Vera Harding makes fun of her husband, flaunts her sexuality, and implies her own infidelity while he is in the hospital. Irony: The prostitutes, Candy and Sandy, are portrayed as good while the women who would ordinarily be viewed as "good," i.e., wives and mothers, are portrayed as manipulating, corrupt women. For example, Billy's mother destroys him sexually, but Candy gives him sexual confidence.)*

7. Discuss the importance of minor characters in the novel and how they advance the plot. *(Sefelt: Nurse Ratched's reaction to his refusal to take his medication for epilepsy reveals one form of her control, i.e., pointing out effects of disobedience; Nurse Pilbow: Ratched suggests to her that McMurphy is a sex maniac. Her guilt and shame because of a birthmark indicate sexual repression; Nurse on the Disturbed Ward: serves as a foil for Ratched because of her gentleness and compassion; Sorensen: his fear of germs and reaction to the forced shower set the stage for McMurphy's attack on Washington and the ensuing events; Mr. Turkle: makes possible the Saturday night party; Candy and Sandy: foils for Ratched and give an example of irony, i.e., the "bad" girls are better than the "good" women; Ellis and Ruckly: examples of mistakes in treatment of mentally ill; Cheswick and Rawler: deaths demonstrate results of Ratched's control.)*

8. Analyze the symbolism of the fog, the EST table and probes used for the treatment, Nurse Ratched's name, the Combine, and McMurphy's ripping of Ratched's uniform. *(Fog: Bromden's escape mechanism where he can hide when threatened; other patients live in a mental fog caused by Ratched, e.g., they cannot think for themselves or act independently. McMurphy brings "light" into the ward, causing the fog to lift. EST: the table—a cross used for crucifixion; the probes—a crown of thorns; both symbolize McMurphy's sacrificial death. Ratched's name: a play on two words, "ratchet" and "wretched." A ratchet is a set of teeth on a bar wheel allowing motion in only one direction, symbolizing her drive to have things her own way. Wretched means very bad or miserable, symbolizing her characteristics. Combine: government and society in general because they control everyone, e.g., the destruction of the Indians' way of life by overpowering and making them small; the hospital because of its control over the men, e.g., Bromden's hallucinations about hidden machinery in the hospital symbolize the hospital's covert methods of controlling the patients. Ripping of Ratched's uniform: exposure of her repressed sexuality and her vulnerability)*

9. Compare/contrast McMurphy and Bromden. *(Comparison: both served in Armed Services and experienced frightful things, are committed in a mental hospital, and receive EST. Contrast: McMurphy rarely ceases speaking; at first Bromden never speaks. McMurphy thinks clearly; Bromden is rarely lucid. McMurphy is strong; Bromden believes he is weak. McMurphy is sane; Bromden is insane. McMurphy faces conflict; Bromden retreats into a mental fog when threatened. In the resolution of the novel, Bromden becomes strong enough to smother McMurphy and escape from the hospital; thus, McMurphy dies and Bromden lives.)*

10. Analyze whether or not Kesey portrays existentialism in the novel. *(McMurphy exemplifies some facets of existentialism, e.g., human choice is subjective because individuals must make their own choices without help from external standards such as laws or ethical rules; because they freely choose, they alone are completely responsible for their actions. No one forces McMurphy to become a martyr for the patients, and he blames no one for his choice. In his hope to effect change, he relinquishes his basic human nature and acts contrary to what would be expected of him.)*

Post-reading Extension Activities

Writing

1. Rewrite one scene from the novel from Nurse Ratched's point of view.

2. Rewrite the story in a poem of at least 24 lines.

3. Write the next chapter of the novel in which Chief Bromden is experiencing life outside the mental hospital.

Drama/Music

4. Write and stage your favorite scene from the novel. Select appropriate background music.

Research

5. Research and write a three- to four-page paper about the types of treatment for mental illness over the past 100 years.

Viewing

6. View the movie, *One Flew Over the Cuckoo's Nest*, and present an oral report to the class comparing/contrasting the actors' portrayals of McMurphy and Bromden with the way the author portrays them in the novel.

Art

7. Draw a caricature of Billy Bibbit.

8. Design and make a two-faced papier-mâché mask showing the "real" Nurse Ratched and the façade behind which she hides.

9. Create a collage depicting the oppression of the mental ward under Nurse Ratched's control.

10. Create a collage depicting Geever, Washington, and Williams, the three black hospital aides under Nurse Ratched's control.

Interviewing

11. Invite a mental health employee to present information on his/her career. Ask questions, based on situations found in the novel. Write a summary of what you learned from the interview.

Assessment for *One Flew Over the Cuckoo's Nest*

Assessment is an ongoing process. The following ten items can be completed during the novel study. Once finished, the student and teacher will check the work. Points may be added to indicate the level of understanding.

Name _____ Date _____

Student   **Teacher**

_____   _____   1. Correct all quizzes and tests for review.

_____   _____   2. Write a review question over each of the four parts of the novel. Participate in an oral review.

_____   _____   3. Write a riddle about one of the characters. Exchange with a partner and identify the character in his or her riddle.

_____   _____   4. Display or perform your Post-reading Extension Activity on the assigned day.

_____   _____   5. Write a review of *One Flew Over the Cuckoo's Nest* for the school newspaper.

_____   _____   6. Choose five chronological events in the novel. Write the beginning of the event on a sheet of paper, exchange with a partner, and complete each other's list.

_____   _____   7. Rewrite the scene in which McMurphy attends his first Group Meeting, from McMurphy's point of view.

_____   _____   8. Compare your completed Character Charts, Story Maps, and Post-reading Extension Activities in groups of three or four.

_____   _____   9. Create a pictorial representation of Dale Harding's character. Use your own illustrations or pictures cut out from magazines and/or newspapers.

_____   _____   10. Identify the types of conflict in the novel.

Glossary

Part One, pp. 9–41
1. cagey (10): shrewd and cautious
2. psychopath (18): a person having a personality disorder characterized by antisocial behavior, indifference to morality, and abnormal changes in mood and activity
3. therapeutic (19): of or having to do with treating or curing disease
4. bent (24): a natural inclination; tendency
5. philosophy (29): broad, general principles of a particular subject or field of activity
6. neurology (31): study of the nervous system and its diseases

pp. 42–69
1. insubordination (44): resistance to authority; refusal to obey
2. protocol (47): rules for any procedure
3. prototype (48): the first or primary type of something; original
4. sadistic (56): relating to sadism (practice of a person who gets pleasure from hurting someone else); an unnatural love of cruelty
5. veritable (58): true, real, or actual; having all the qualities or attributes of a specified person or thing
6. ethereally (58): airily; delicately
7. benevolence (58): desire to promote the happiness of others; kindness
8. matriarchy (59): government by women
9. astute (61): shrewd, especially with regard to one's own interests; crafty
10. juggernaut (66): a frightening, invisible force that destroys anything in its path
11. impregnable (67): cannot be overthrown by force; unconquerable

pp. 70–101
1. stoicism (73): patient endurance; indifference to pleasure or pain
2. uncanny (75): strange, mysterious, or eerie
3. geriatrics (89): branch of medicine dealing with the study of aging
4. infernal (95): outrageous, detestable, or abominable
5. maudlin (97): sentimental in a weak, silly way; overemotional

pp. 102–128
1. apathy (107): lack of interest, concern, or emotion; indifference
2. interceptors (116): fast fighter planes having high rate of climb; used to repel attacking bombers

Part Two, pp. 129–151
1. *arch type (134): original model or pattern from which copies are made; prototype
2. schizophrenic (135): have characteristics of schizophrenia, a form of psychosis in which the patient disconnects himself from his surroundings and mentally and socially deteriorates
3. latent (135): present but not active; concealed
4. Oedipal (135): having to do with the Oedipus complex (a strong childhood attachment of a male child to his mother)
5. blowhard (136): noisy boaster
6. silage (141): green fodder stored in a silo and preserved by partial fermentation
7. impound (146): to seize or hold back
8. hydrocephalus (149): an accumulation of cerebrospinal fluid within the cranium; often causes great enlargement of the head
9. lymph (149): a nearly colorless liquid present in body tissue

*spelling in novel

pp. 152–173
1. kneading (153): shaping with the hands
2. schematic (157): having to do with or like a diagram
3. curtail (158): cut short; diminish
4. nemesis (158): agent of retribution; doom
5. punitive (163): seeking to punish; inflicting punishment
6. lobotomy (163): surgical incision into a lobe of the human brain, especially to cut nerve fibers in the treatment of certain mental disorders
7. aplomb (163): complete confidence in oneself; self-assurance
8. vogue (164): popularity, acceptance, or prevalence
9. lucid (165): clear in intellect; sane; rational
10. spoor (169): trail of a wild animal or person
11. circumvent (171): go around; avoid

Part Three, pp. 174–190
1. hovel (180): small, crude house that is unpleasant to live in
2. fraternize (180): associate with in a friendly way
3. squalor (180): misery and dirt; filth
4. indigents (189): poor or needy persons

pp. 191–218
1. keelhaul (192): to haul a person under the keel of a ship for punishment
2. wistful (192): longing, yearning
3. turret (204): revolving, armored structure in which guns are mounted
4. cormorants (210): very large sea birds

Part Four, pp. 219–241
1. philanthropy (222): love of mankind shown by practical kindness and helpfulness to humanity; benevolence
2. capitalistic (223): favoring or supporting capitalism (the concentration of wealth with its power and influence in the hands of a few); entrepreneurial
3. chicanery (223): low trickery; deception; unfair practices
4. effrontery (223): shameless boldness; impudence

pp. 242–259
1. provocative (248): something that rouses, stimulates, or irritates
2. chastising (258): inflicting punishment; criticizing or rebuking severely

pp. 260–272
1. shellacked (261): varnished with an alcohol-based substance that gives a smooth, shiny appearance
2. atrocities (262): acts of great cruelty or wickedness
3. discretion (264): quality of having good judgment in speech or action
4. contemptuous (265): scornful, disdainful
5. skittered (268): moved lightly or quickly
6. syndicate (272): a group that organizes and controls criminal activities